P9-AFT-297

Fishman, Jon M.,
Khalil Mack /
[2021]

cu   06/08/21

Lerner SPORTS

SPORTS
ALL-ST★RS

KHALIL MACK

Jon M. Fishman

Lerner Publications ◆ Minneapolis

SCORE BIG with sports fans, reluctant readers, and report writers!

Lerner Sports is a database of high-interest biographies profiling notable sports superstars. Packed with fascinating facts, these bios explore the backgrounds, career-defining moments, and everyday lives of popular athletes. Lerner Sports is perfect for young readers developing research skills or looking for exciting sports content.

LERNER SPORTS FEATURES:
- ☑ Keyword search
- ☑ Topic navigation menus
- ☑ Fast facts
- ☑ Related bio suggestions to encourage more reading
- ☑ Admin view of reader statistics
- ☑ Fresh content updated regularly

and more!

Visit LernerSports.com for a free trial!

 Lerner SPORTS

Copyright © 2021 by Lerner Publishing Group, Inc.

All rights reserved. International copyright secured. No part of this book may be reproduced, stored in a retrieval system, or transmitted in any form or by any means—electronic, mechanical, photocopying, recording, or otherwise—without the prior written permission of Lerner Publishing Group, Inc., except for the inclusion of brief quotations in an acknowledged review.

Lerner Publications Company
An imprint of Lerner Publishing Group, Inc.
241 First Avenue North
Minneapolis, MN 55401 USA

For reading levels and more information, look up this title at www.lernerbooks.com.

Main body text set in Albany Std 22. Typeface provided by Agfa.

Editor: Shee Yang

Library of Congress Cataloging-in-Publication Data

Names: Fishman, Jon M., author.
Title: Khalil Mack / Jon M. Fishman.
Description: Minneapolis, MN : Lerner Publications, 2021 | Series: Sports all-stars (Lerner sports) | Includes bibliographical references and index. | Audience: Ages 7–11 | Audience: Grades 2–3 | Summary: "From his career with the Oakland Raiders to becoming the highest paid defensive player in NFL history with the Chicago Bears, Khalil Mack has always been a standout. Readers will love his amazing story!"— Provided by publisher.
Identifiers: LCCN 2020000494 (print) | LCCN 2020000495 (ebook) | ISBN 9781541597495 (library binding) | ISBN 9781728414027 (paperback) | ISBN 9781728400983 (ebook)
Subjects: LCSH: Mack, Khalil, 1991-—Juvenile literature. | Football players—United States—Biography—Juvenile literature. | Linebackers (Football)—United States—Biography—Juvenile literature.
Classification: LCC GV939.M227 F57 2021 (print) | LCC GV939.M227 (ebook) | DDC 796.332092 [B]—dc23

LC record available at https://lccn.loc.gov/2020000494
LC ebook record available at https://lccn.loc.gov/2020000495

Manufactured in the United States of America
1-47853-48293-4/1/2020

CONTENTS

MACK ATTACK

Khalil Mack (left) tackles Case Keenum in the first quarter of a game on September 23, 2019.

Washington Redskins quarterback Case Keenum stepped back with the ball. He faked a hand off to his running back. Keenum turned to look for an open receiver, but all he saw was Chicago Bears **linebacker** Khalil Mack.

- **Date of birth:** February 22, 1991

- **Position:** linebacker

- **League:** National Football League (NFL)

- **Professional highlights:** chosen with the fifth overall pick in the 2014 NFL Draft; won the 2016 NFL Defensive Player of the Year award; became the highest-paid defensive player in NFL history

- **Personal highlights:** grew up in Fort Pierce, Florida; in high school, dreamed of becoming a star basketball player; played just one year of high school football

Mack streaked across the **line of scrimmage**. He zoomed past Washington players who stood in his way. Keenum had no chance. Mack wrapped his powerful arms around the quarterback and dragged him to the ground for a **sack**.

Mack and the Bears were playing in Washington, DC, on September 23, 2019. The sack helped Chicago hold onto a 7–0 lead in the first quarter. By the second quarter, the Bears had extended the lead to 14–0. That's when Mack struck again.

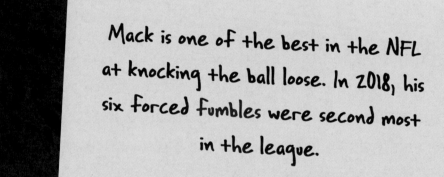

Mack is one of the best in the NFL at knocking the ball loose. In 2018, his six forced fumbles were second most in the league.

Mack celebrates a good play in September 2018.

Keenum stepped back to pass, but Mack charged at him. At the last moment, a Washington player pushed Mack past Keenum. But the linebacker reached out with his right arm and swatted the ball out of Keenum's grasp. Chicago recovered the fumble as Mack danced on the field.

The Bears kept piling on the points to beat Washington 31–15. Mack had four tackles and two sacks in the game. It was another excellent performance for the linebacker. Since he joined the NFL in 2014, no other defender in football has made a bigger impact on the game.

CHANGING PLANS

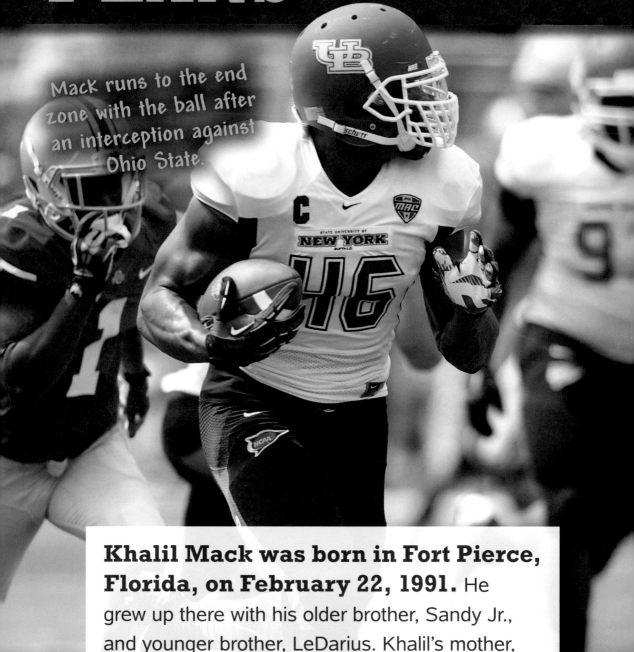

Mack runs to the end zone with the ball after an interception against Ohio State.

Khalil Mack was born in Fort Pierce, Florida, on February 22, 1991. He grew up there with his older brother, Sandy Jr., and younger brother, LeDarius. Khalil's mother, Yolanda Mack, was an elementary school

Fort Pierce, Florida

teacher. Sandy Mack Sr., Khalil's father, worked with young people in the Florida legal system.

The Mack brothers loved to compete with one another. Their father encouraged them. "I taught my boys how to be competitive," the elder Mack said. "We like to win." They played sports such as football, basketball, and bowling. And they always played to win.

Mack (*right*) laughs with two of his Westwood High School teammates.

Khalil played football at a park near his house with kids from the neighborhood. During those games, he learned that he liked tackling other players better than he liked being tackled. That realization shaped the rest of his football career.

As he grew older, Khalil began playing basketball more often than other sports. By the time he reached Westwood High School, he dreamed of earning a college basketball **scholarship**. But in his sophomore year, he injured his knee during a game.

By the time Khalil became a senior at Westwood, his knee was finally healthy again. But his focus had shifted to football. He racked up 140 tackles and nine sacks in the 2008–2009 season. He helped Westwood attain a 10–2 record.

Khalil's senior season should have been good enough to earn several college football scholarship offers. But since he had played only one year of **varsity** football, many college coaches didn't know much about him. Khalil received just two offers, from the University at Buffalo in New York and Liberty University in Virginia. Both schools were in small **conferences** that didn't get a lot of attention from fans.

The Buffalo Bulls didn't have much success when Mack played for the team. From 2010 to 2013, the Bulls had a poor 17—32 record.

Mack tackles the Ohio State quarterback during a game in Columbus, Ohio.

Mack chose Buffalo. The weather in western New York was a lot colder than it was in Florida. But the new climate didn't affect his play. In his four seasons with the Buffalo Bulls, Mack averaged more than seven sacks per year. In 2013, he won the Mid-American Conference Defensive Player of the Year award. He was ready for the NFL.

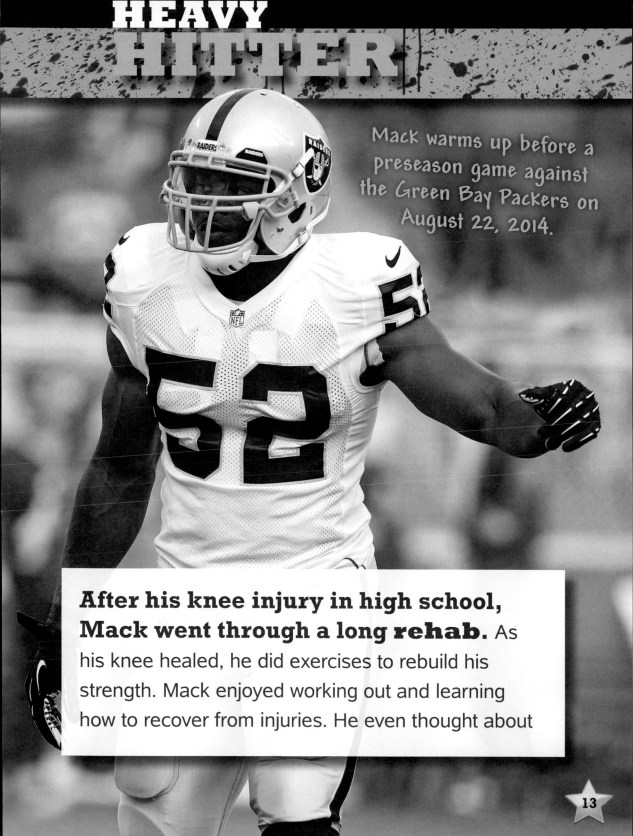

Mack warms up before a preseason game against the Green Bay Packers on August 22, 2014.

After his knee injury in high school, Mack went through a long rehab. As his knee healed, he did exercises to rebuild his strength. Mack enjoyed working out and learning how to recover from injuries. He even thought about becoming a **physical therapist** after college.

When his knee was healthy again, Mack didn't stop working out. He hit the gym harder than ever. Mack starts his workouts with stretching exercises that help him move more easily and reach farther. When his body feels ready for the tough stuff, the real work begins. Mack targets his muscle groups with different workouts. He pushes a

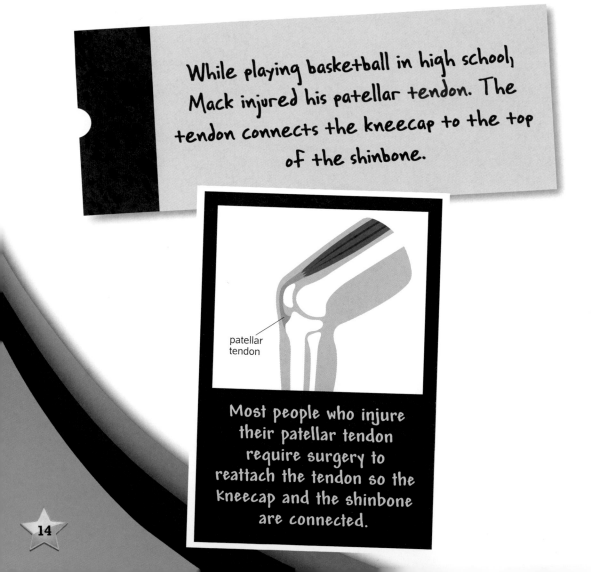

While playing basketball in high school, Mack injured his patellar tendon. The tendon connects the kneecap to the top of the shinbone.

patellar tendon

Most people who injure their patellar tendon require surgery to reattach the tendon so the kneecap and the shinbone are connected.

Mack stretches before practice on May 16, 2014.

heavy exercise sled to toughen his legs. He lifts heavy
weights to strengthen his arms, chest, and shoulders.

Not all of Mack's exercises require workout equipment.
He does a lot of push-ups and sit-ups. He runs on grass
fields, quickly cutting left and right as if he's chasing a

Players push heavy blocking sleds to build strength and practice pushing other players around the field.

quarterback. He also runs barefoot on sand. Mack's feet sink in, forcing him to work harder for every inch.

In his first NFL season, Mack weighed about 250 pounds (113 kg). One year later, he weighed 270 pounds (123 kg).

Mack's workouts get his body ready for NFL games. To get his mind ready, he watches videos. "I'm always looking at film, studying myself, comparing and contrasting with film of the great linebackers to see what I need to work on," Mack said. He also watches recordings of upcoming opponents. He looks for weaknesses and makes plans to take advantage of them.

Mack chases the quarterback during a 2019 game against the Philadelphia Eagles.

BEAR HUG

Mack celebrates with fans after
beating the Green Bay Packers
on December 16, 2018.

Mack holds his new Oakland Raiders jersey after the team chose him in the 2014 NFL Draft.

In college, Mack became one of the hardest-hitting defenders in football.

He often crushed ballcarriers behind the line of scrimmage, causing the opposing team to lose yards. His 75 career tackles for loss were the most in college history. In 2014, the Oakland Raiders chose him with the fifth overall pick in the NFL Draft.

Mack poses with his Bears jersey on September 2, 2018.

Mack played four seasons in Oakland. In September 2018, the Raiders traded him to Chicago. Right away, Mack and the Bears agreed to a six-year contract worth $141 million. The deal made him the highest-paid defender in NFL history.

Soon after the trade, Mack bought a house in Chicago. The $3.75 million home has six bedrooms, a theater, and a library. It also has four fireplaces to help keep Mack warm during cold Chicago winters.

Bears fans fell in love with Mack. Signs appeared around the city welcoming him to Chicago. At home games, fans wearing Mack jerseys seemed to be everywhere, and people recognized him wherever he went.

Mack uses his money and popularity to improve Chicago and other communities. The Khalil Mack Foundation is dedicated to helping struggling communities. Besides providing money to groups that help people in need, the foundation organizes sports activities and provides safe spaces for kids to play and learn.

Mack greets happy fans after a victory against the Detroit Lions.

Mack also works with his teammates to give back. In 2018, he wore special shoes during a game to increase awareness of **lupus**. The next summer, he played in an all-star softball game to raise money for Goodwill and the Remain to Reach Foundation, which works to provide resources for children and help them create paths to success.

Football players often show support for causes by having special shoes made. They wear them to games to spread awareness.

Secret Santa

Some stores have layaway programs. Layaway lets a customer make payments to a store toward the purchase of an item. When all the payments are made, the store hands the item over to the customer.

In December 2019, Mack surprised some customers at a Walmart in Fort Pierce. Through the Khalil Mack Foundation, he donated $80,000 to pay for layaways for more than 300 customers. "His foundation came to us and said he wanted to be a secret Santa," the store's manager said.

Mack treated hundreds of Walmart shoppers to a holiday surprise by paying for their purchases in December 2019.

SUPER GOAL

Mack during a September 2016 game against the Atlanta Falcons

Mack was good in his first NFL season. In 2014, he recorded four sacks and 16 tackles for loss with Oakland. He learned a lot about playing professionally and decided if he wanted to be the best, he had to become stronger and faster.

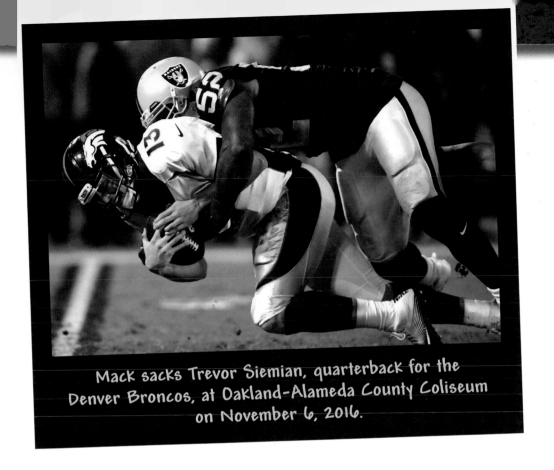

Mack sacks Trevor Siemian, quarterback for the Denver Broncos, at Oakland-Alameda County Coliseum on November 6, 2016.

After packing on 20 pounds (9 kg) of muscle between 2014 and 2015, Mack became an unstoppable defensive force. In 2015, he finished second in the NFL with 15 sacks. He also had an incredible 23 tackles for loss.

In 2016, Mack won the Defensive Player of the Year award with 11 sacks and 73 tackles. He was almost as good in 2017. But rumors spread that the Raiders were trying to trade Mack to another team.

Mack tackles Philadelphia Eagles quarterback Nick Foles during the NFC Wild Card game on January 6, 2019.

Mack's incredible play deserved a big pay raise. But NFL teams have limits on how much they can pay players. The Raiders didn't have as much money to offer Mack as other teams did, so they traded him to the Bears.

Mack made a huge impact on the Chicago defense. With the superstar linebacker leading the way, the team ranked at the top of many defensive stats in 2018. The Bears made the playoffs but lost to the Philadelphia Eagles.

Mack didn't watch the 2019 Super Bowl. Instead, he worked out and thought about the next season. His goal is winning a championship with the Bears. But with 10 other Bears on the field, he can only do so much. "This game is all about making everybody around you great, not so much about making myself great," Mack said. If the rest of the Bears can follow Mack's lead, the Super Bowl trophy will soon return to Chicago.

Chicago beat the New England Patriots in 1986 for the team's only Super Bowl victory. Many fans believe Chicago's defense that year was one of the best in NFL history.

All-Star Stats

The Chicago Bears are one of the NFL's oldest teams. They began playing pro football in the early 1920s. Through all those years, only one player has had more sacks in a season than Khalil Mack had in 2018.

Player	Sacks	Season
Richard Dent	17.5	1984
Richard Dent	17	1985
Khalil Mack	**12.5**	**2018**
Richard Dent	12.5	1993
Richard Dent	12.5	1987
Mark Anderson	12	2006
Richard Dent	12	1990
Mike Hartenstine	12	1983
Julius Peppers	11.5	2012
Trace Armstrong	11.5	1993
Steve McMichael	11.5	1988
Richard Dent	11.5	1986
Dan Hampton	11.5	1984

Glossary

conferences: groups of sports teams

fumbles: instances of losing hold of the football

linebacker: a defensive football player who lines up just behind the line of scrimmage

line of scrimmage: an imaginary line in football that marks the position of the ball at the start of each play

lupus: any of several diseases marked by skin problems

physical therapist: someone who helps people recover from injuries

rehab: a program of exercise and therapy designed to help a person recover from injury

sack: tackling the quarterback behind the line of scrimmage

scholarship: money given to students to help pay for school

tendon: a tough cord or band that connects a muscle with a bone

varsity: the top team at a school

Source Notes

9   Jason Leskiw, "Raiders Newest Linebacker Khalil Mack Comes from Humble Beginnings," Medium, May 10, 2014, https://medium.com/@LeskiwSFBay/raiders-newest -linebacker-khalil-mack-comes-from-humble-beginnings -afe4361d523b.

17 Matthew Jussim, "Here's How Khalil Mack Trains to Dominate the NFL," *Men's Journal*, accessed December 14, 2019, https://www.mensjournal.com/sports/heres-how -khalil-mack-training-dominate-nfl-again/.

23 Christopher Brito, "NFL Star Khalil Mack Pays Off All $80,000 Worth of Layaways at Hometown Walmart," CBS News, December 11, 2019, https://www.cbsnews.com /news/khalil-mack-layaway-fort-pierce-florida-chicago -bears-nfl/.

27 Tim Daniels, "Khalil Mack Says There Needs to Be Sense of Urgency for Bears: 'Gotta Win Now,'" Bleacher Report, July 31, 2019, https://bleacherreport.com/articles /2847875-khalil-mack-says-there-needs-to-be -sense-of-urgency-for-bears-gotta-win-now.

Further Information

Football: National Football League
http://www.ducksters.com/sports/national_football_league.php

Khalil Mack
https://thekhalilmack.com/

Monson, James. *Behind the Scenes Football*. Minneapolis: Lerner Publications, 2020.

Osborne, M. K. *Superstars of the Chicago Bears*. Mankato, MN: Amicus, 2019.

Pro Football Reference: Rushing
https://www.pro-football-reference.com/years/2019/rushing.htm

Whiting, Jim. *The Story of the Chicago Bears*. Mankato, MN: Creative, 2020.

Index

Photo Acknowledgments

Image credits: Brian Cassella/Chicago Tribune/Getty Images, pp. 4, 26; Jonathan Daniel/Getty Images, pp. 7, 16, 17, 18, 21; David Dermer/Diamond Images/Getty Images, pp. 8, 12; Sara and Joe Williams/Shutterstock.com, p. 9; Sarah Grile/The Palm Beach Post/ZUMA Press Inc/Alamy Stock Photo, p. 10; John Konstantaras/ Getty Images, p. 13; Barks_japan/iStock/Getty Images, p. 14; Thearon W. Henderson/Getty Images, pp. 15, 25; Rich Kane/Icon Sports Wire/Getty Images, p. 19; Erin Hooley/Chicago Tribune/Getty Images, p. 20; AP Photo/Paul Sancya, p. 22; Mike Mozart/flickr (CC BY 2.0), p. 23; Jason O. Watson/Getty Images, p. 24. Design element throughout: iconeer/iStock/Getty Images.

Cover: Robin Alam/Icon Sportswire/Getty Images.